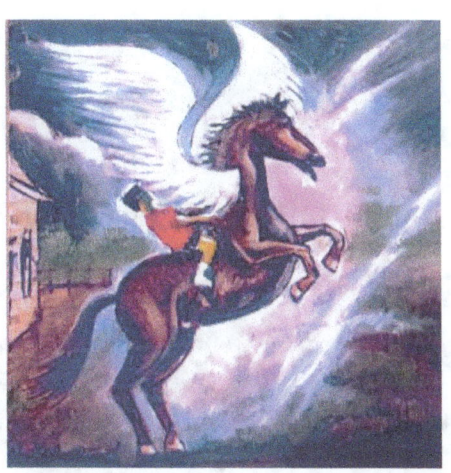

DREAMLAND WORLD

Library of Congress Control Number:

ISBN 978-1-716-22817-9
Printed by Lulu Pree Inc.

www.lulu.com/bookstore

www.amazon.com/books
www.davidgunterstudio.com
Email dgun7000@yahoo.com

Printed in the United States of America 2020

Dedicated

To our Precious Children's who is our future
wealth. We need to treat them as such, Invest in them
with postive Images and words. Stimulate their
inmagnations to help them grow and think creative in
anythings they set out to do.

To My Lovely Wife Carolyn Gunter, Mary J. Clark
Elementary School Teacher. Dearest Mother Julia M.
Gunter, Rev. John L. Gunter, Bennie Bowie, Sophia
Bowie, Karlicha Gunter-Best School Teacher, Tara
Gunter, Mary Gantt
School Teacher, Bessie Bowie, Friends and Kinfolks

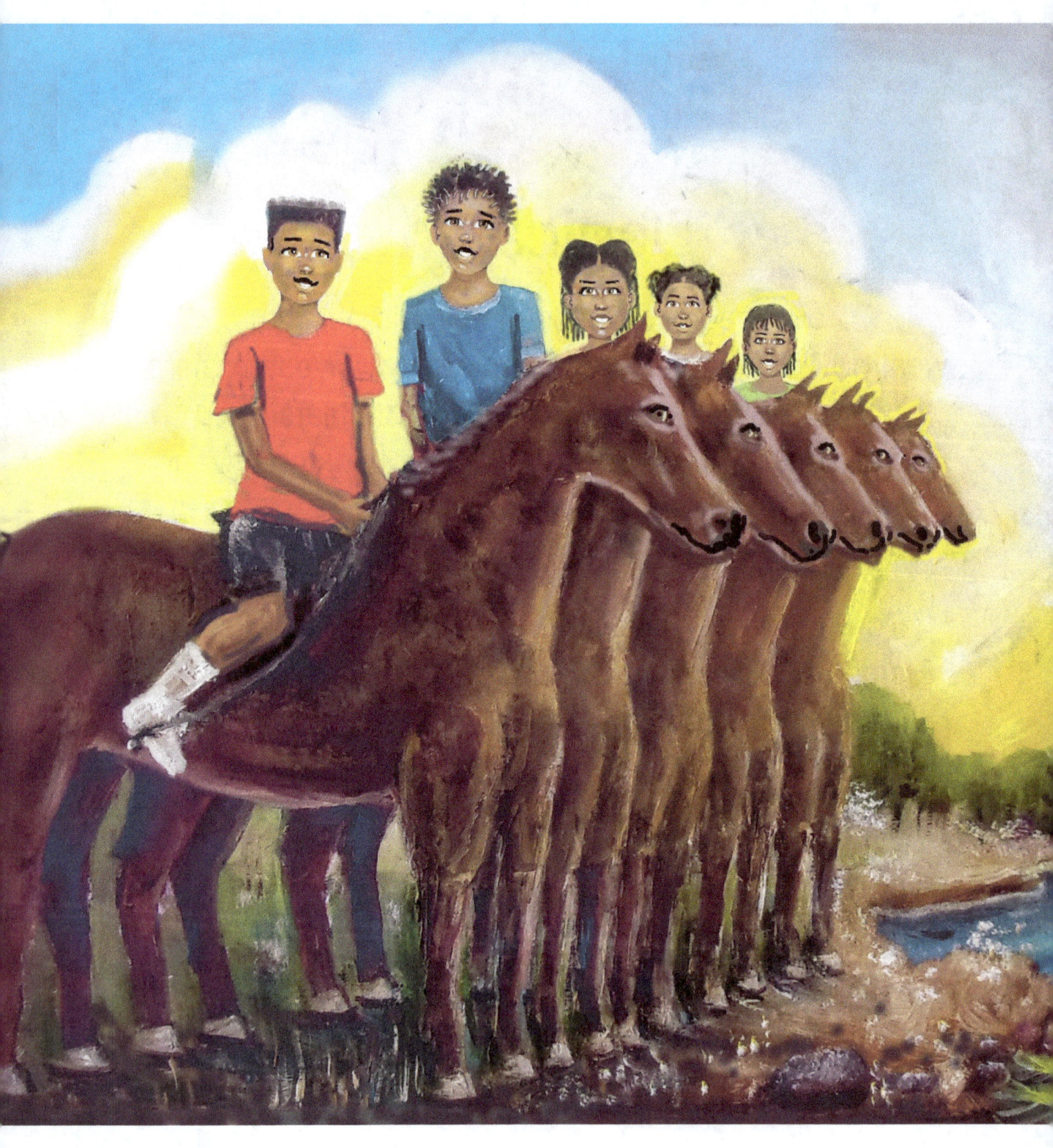

We live on twenty acres of land with a large, beautiful lake. Our house sits back off the main road. A few neighbors live around us at a distance, and mostly keep to themselves. I have one brother, Bubble, and three sisters, Mary, Betty, and Carolyn. I love to ride my horse, Champion. He is one of five horses that my Dad bought. The man that my Dad bought the horses from told him that they were very special. He said, "One day they will bring your kids lots of fun and a fortune." To tell the truth, I believe he was just tired of feeding and caring for them.

When we were out of school during the hot summer months, my big sisters and brother rode their horses very far into the woods, except for me.

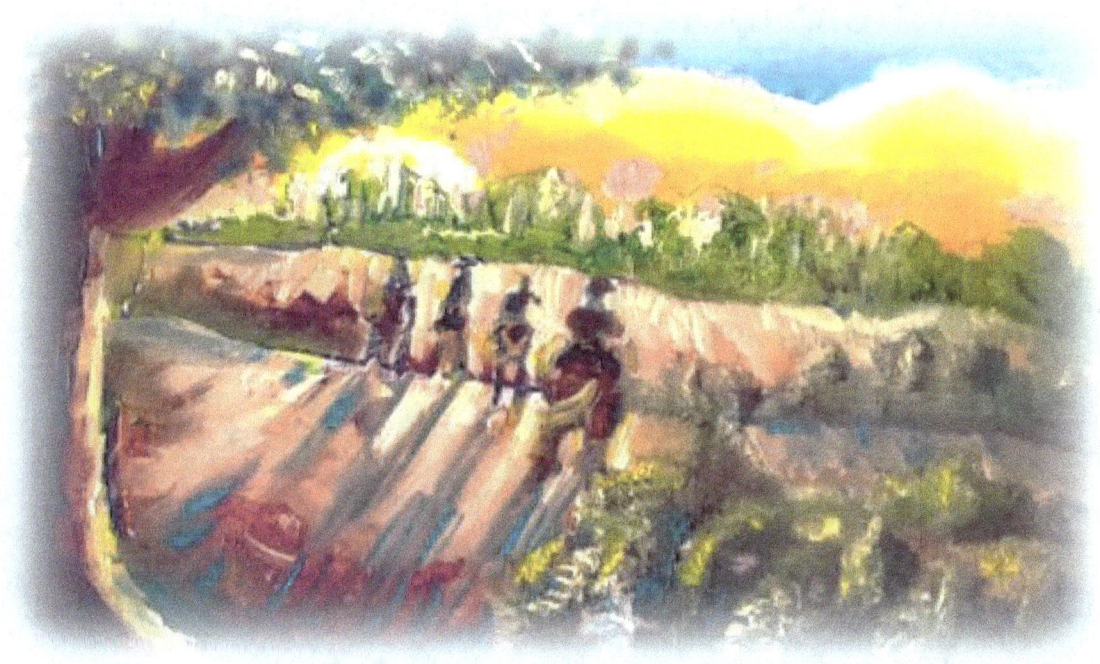

My mother would walk beside my horse to keep me from falling off, because I was too young to ride by myself.

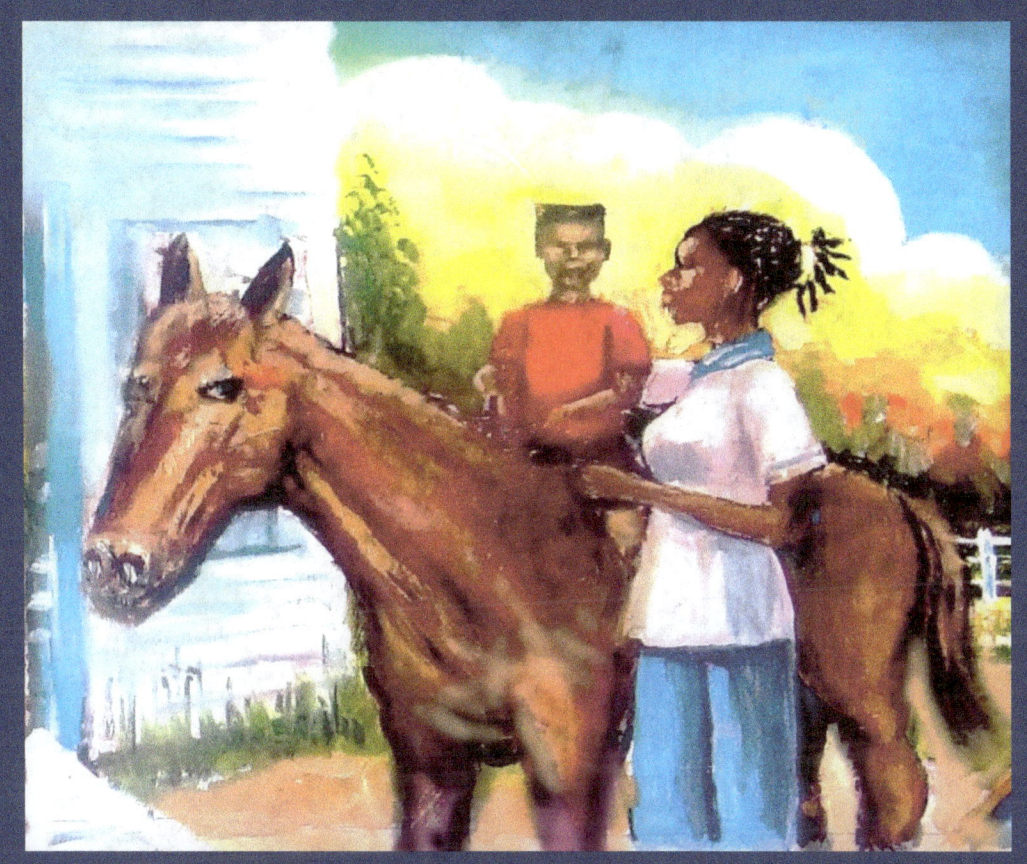

"One day, Samuel you be able to ride with freedom with them," his mother said. "Mommy, when I grow up I will be able to go riding on my own," he replied. "Yes that is right baby, she said," I am not a baby anymore." Laughing, his mother added, "Well, let's just say you are my little man."

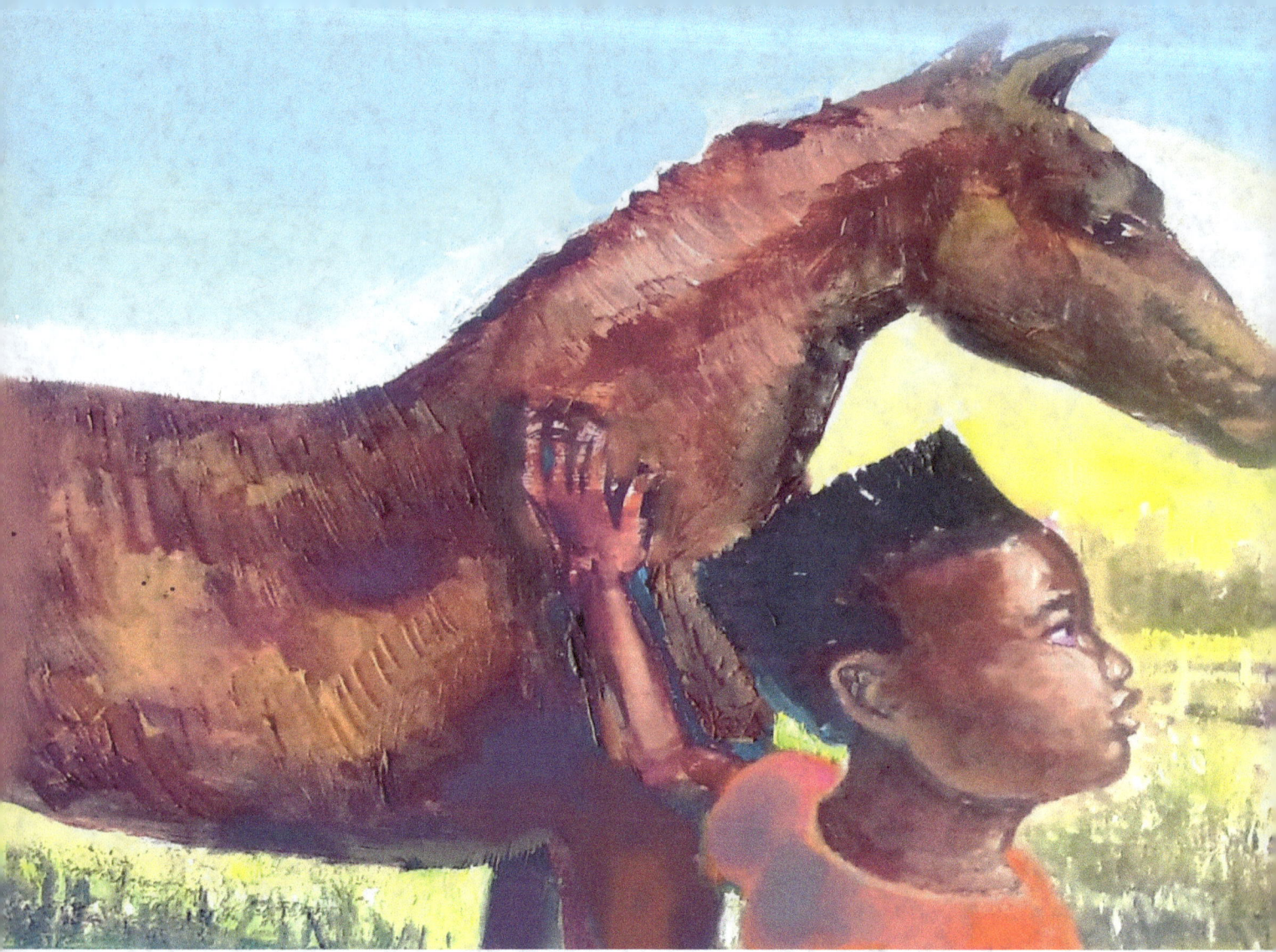

After returning home from their long ride, his brother and sisters were so excited, "Look mom, we found some black berries down by the lake," Mary exclaimed. "Yes," yelled" Bubble, "way back over by those high hills."

"Wash them off first before eating them," their mom warned.

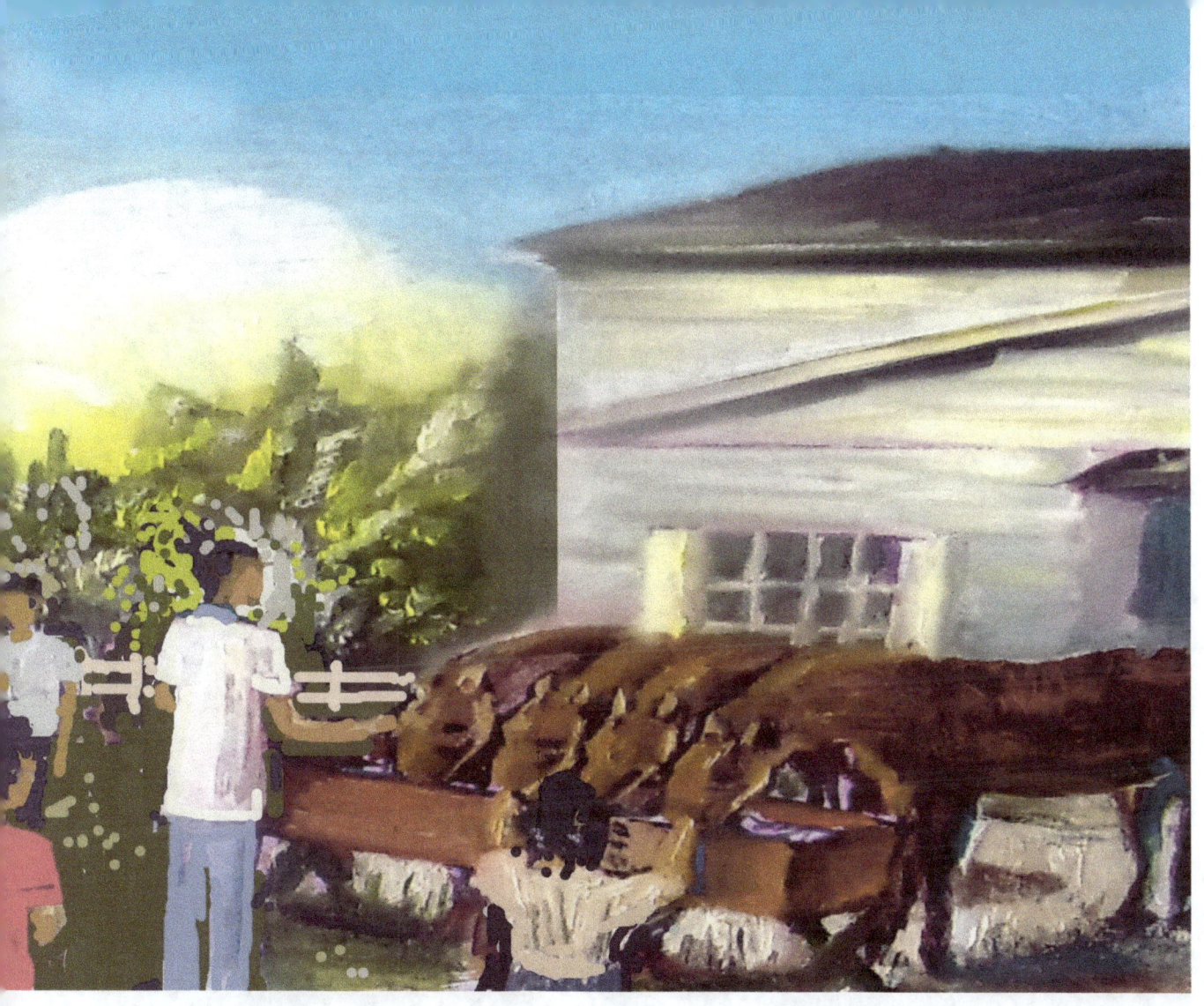

All the horses were tired from the long walk.
The children walked them over to the feeding
area and gave them water. Samuel stood
beside his horse, looking at the horses drink
the water, thinking, one day that he would go
riding with his brother and sisters.

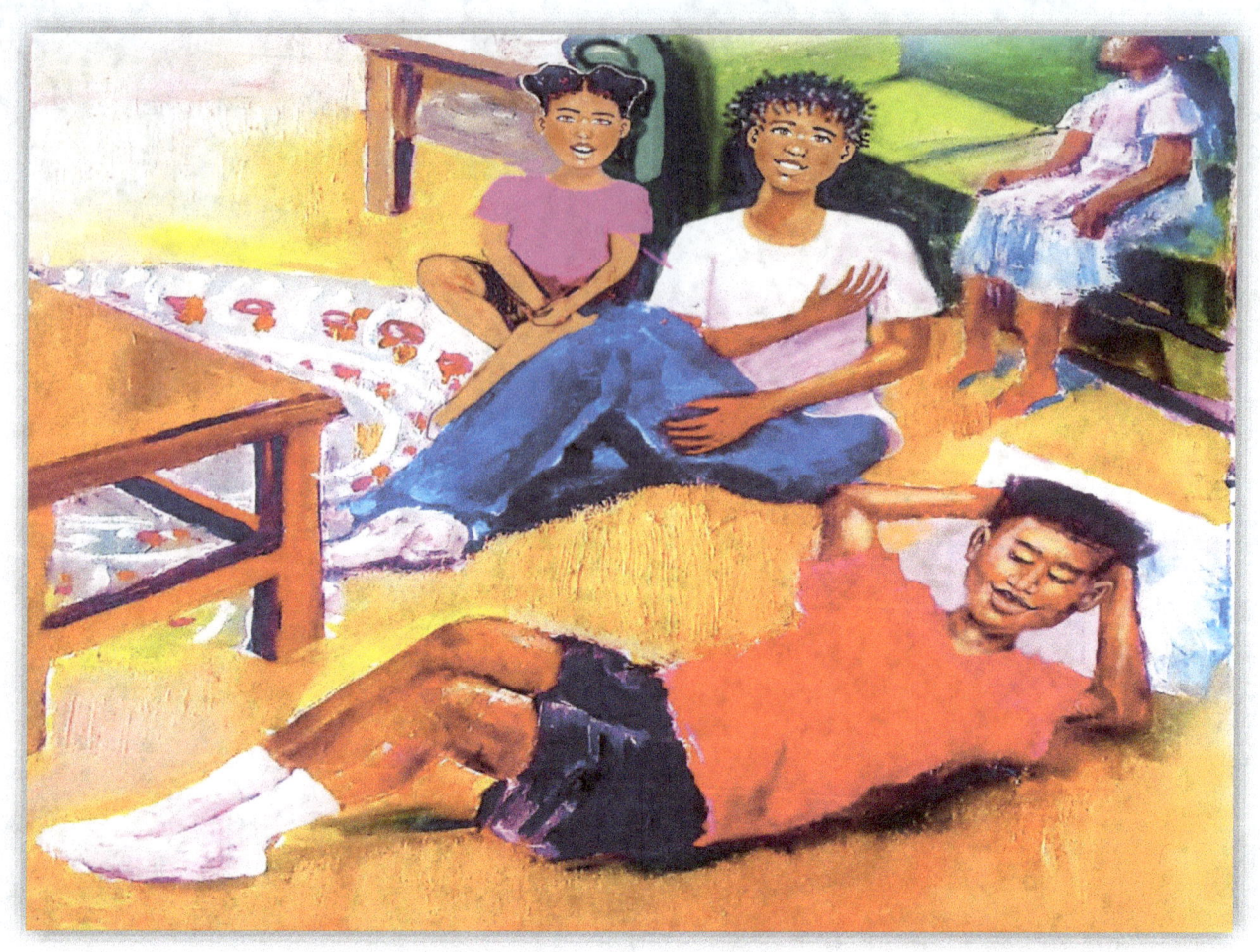

The next summer, Samuel had grown a little taller. He rode in the back woods, but wanted more excitement riding his horse. Back at the house one night, Bubble and his sisters were talking. Soon, Samuel fell asleep on the carpet floor and started to dream.

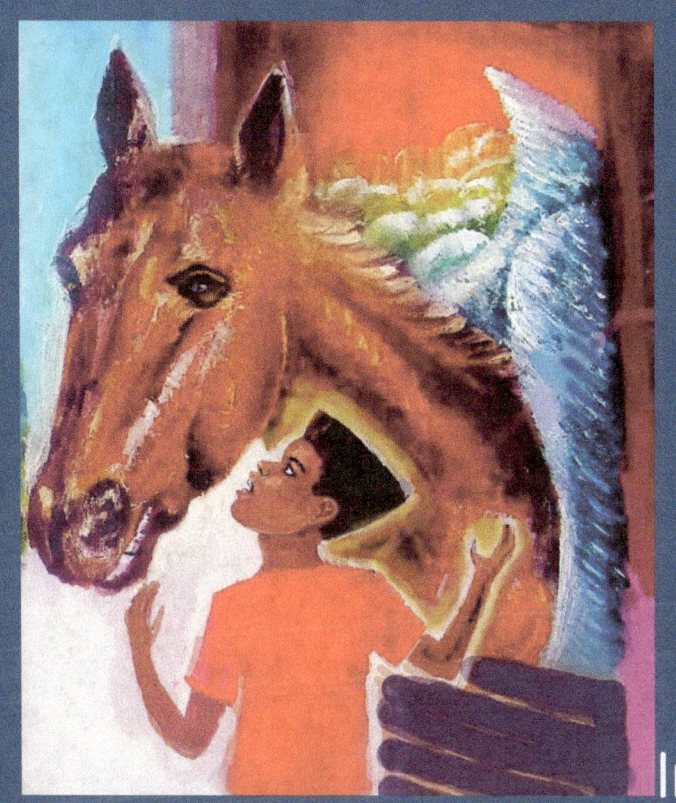

In his dream, he walked to the barn and took his horse out of the stable. "Do not forget you have to ask your parents' permission to ride," Champion said," "You are sounding like my dad, I'm a big boy now don't you see?" "Yes, but I do not want to be blamed if you fall and get hurt. Your parents will get rid of me. I care and love living here in this big barn with my horse friends and you all too. I can take you to a fun place call Dreamland World." "Well I guess you're right; I will go ask my parents if I can go with you." He rushed to the house in the rain, and returned shortly. "Dad said I could go, but I have to be back in thirty minutes." "Well good," said the horse.

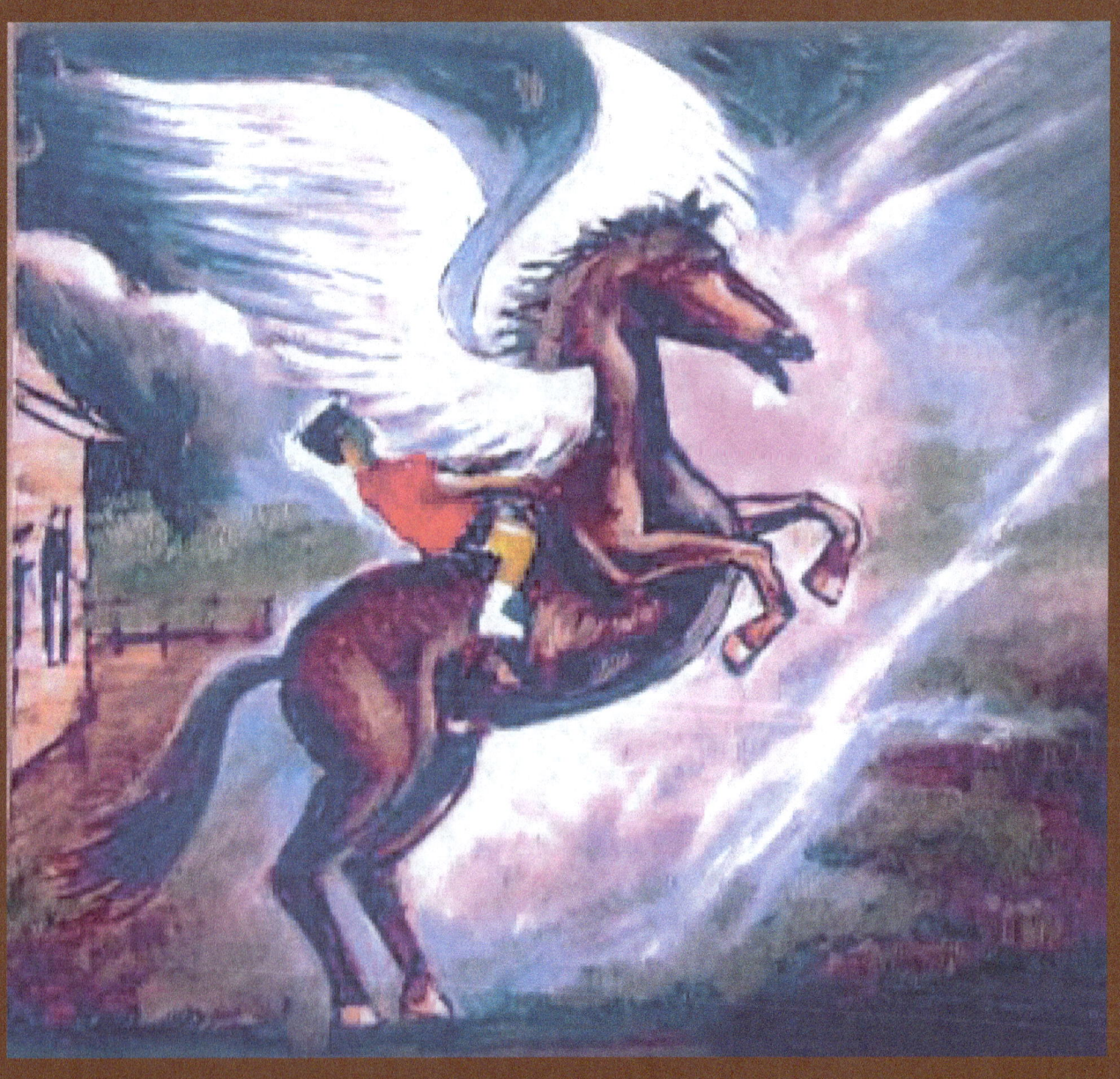

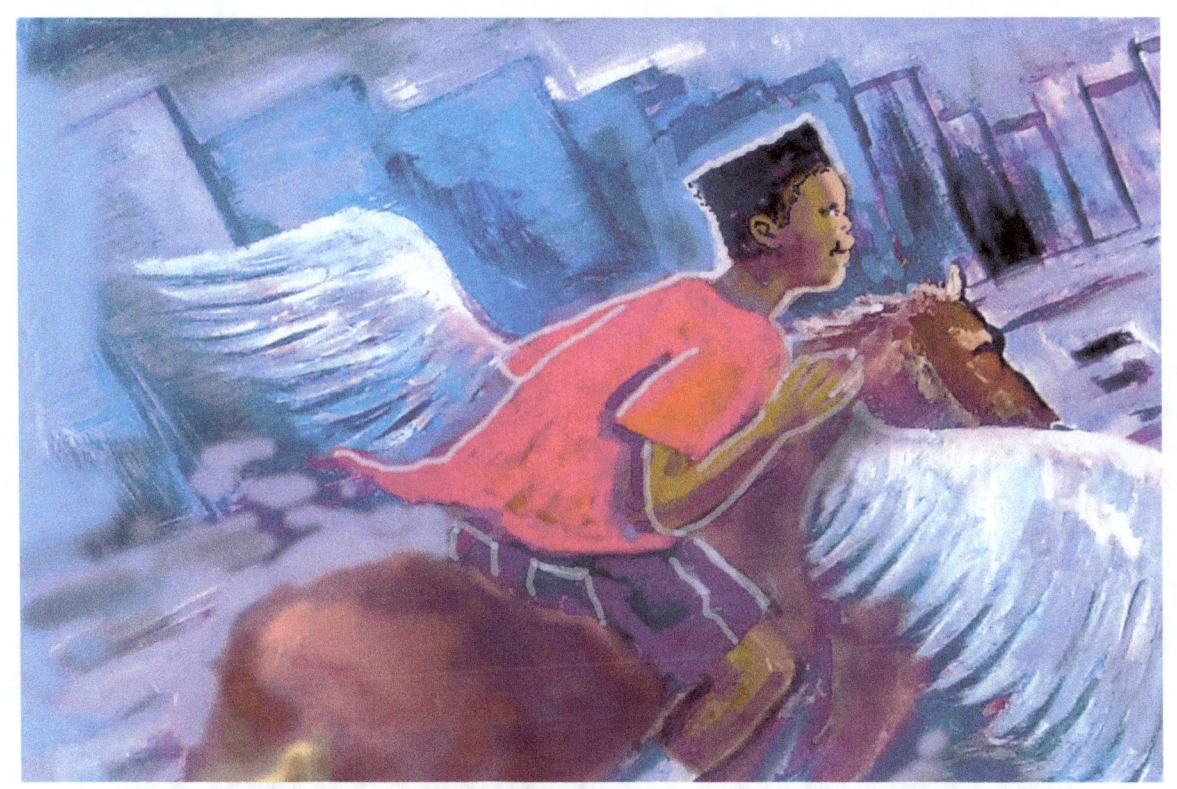

"Ok, Samuel, enough talking, saddle up and let us go up town. You have to ride tall in the saddle." It had been raining with loud thunder, and lots of lightning. However, when they were ready to go, the rain stopped and the sky turned darker blue. After Samuel got on the horse, its body changed. All of a sudden, large folded wings came from both sides of Champion, and he leaped up high off the ground. The wings stretched out wide; soon they were flying in the air high above the uptown lights below.

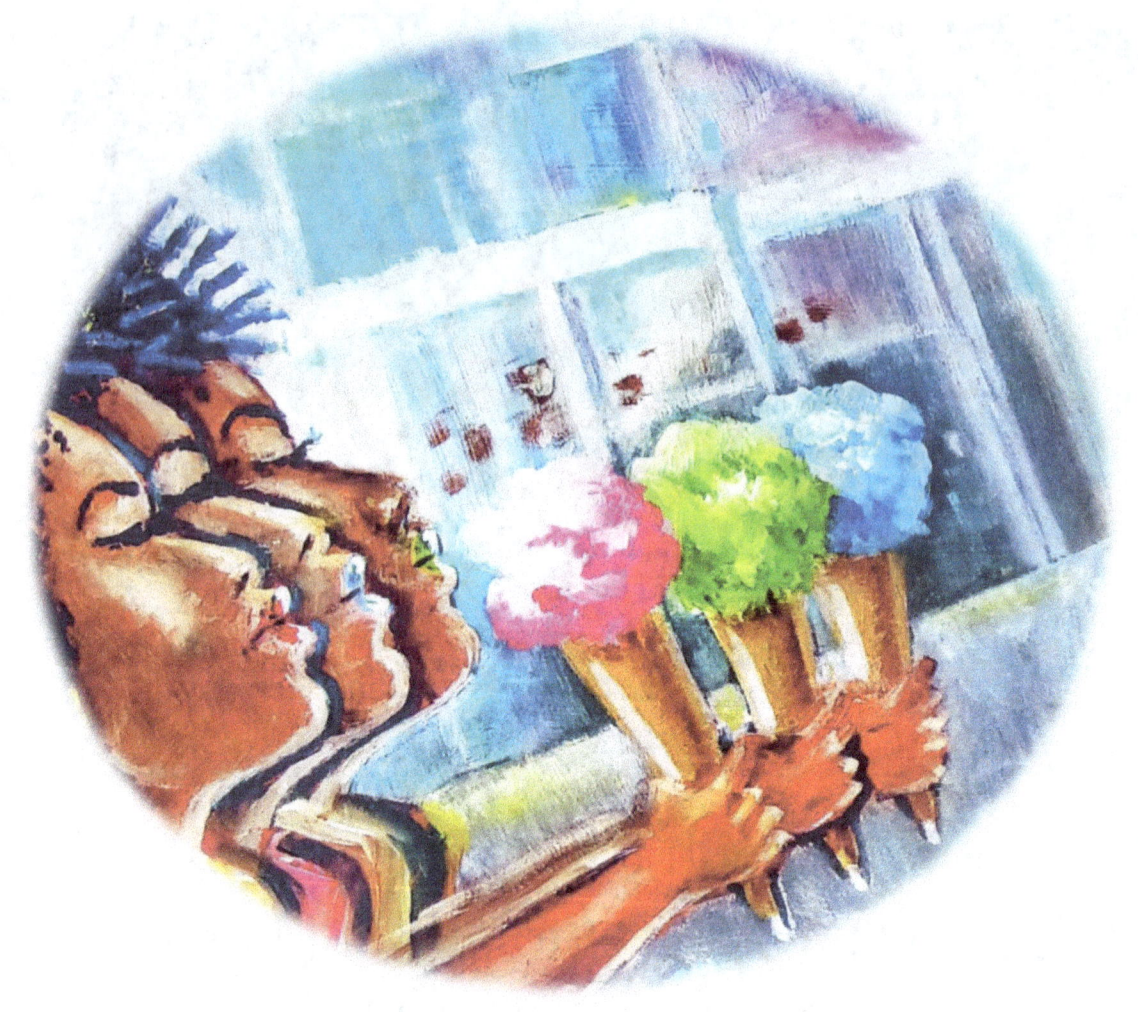

The horse landed on an uptown street and he and Samuel began to explore the area. Samuel decided to go to an ice cream bar for a cone of his favorite flavor, chocolate. There were some little girls standing at the bar, and he bought them some ice cream too. They all waved him goodbye as he and Champion continued their walk.

.

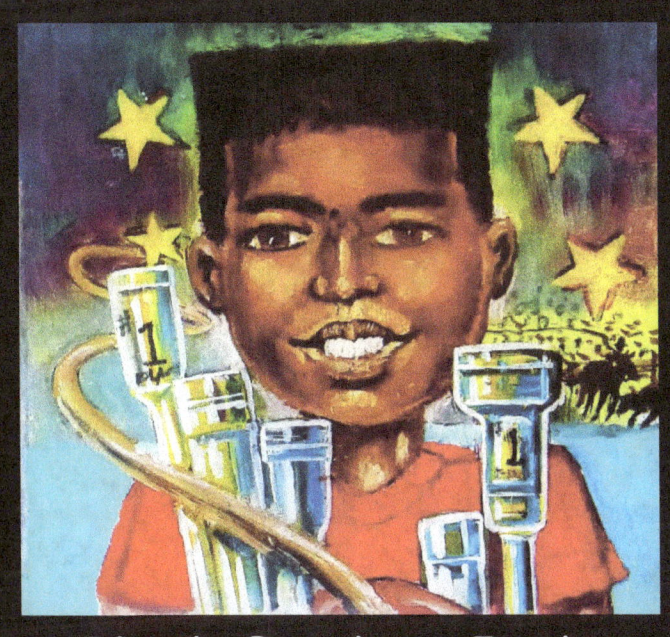

Samuel and Champion
went to the National
Black Cowboy Rodeo that night. "Let's go win
a few trophies," urged Champion. "Okay, if you
think we can win, I will try," replied Samuel who
was not sure that he would be able to win
anything. The horse noticed that Samuel was
not confident, and wanted him to think positive.
"No son, don't think defeat before we start,
this is your night to succeed," said Champion,
encouragingly. They entered the contest and
ended up winning five grand prizes. Samuel
was happy and glad that the horse encouraged
him to try. "Are you ready to go home now?"
Champion asked.

Samuel was definitely not ready to end his

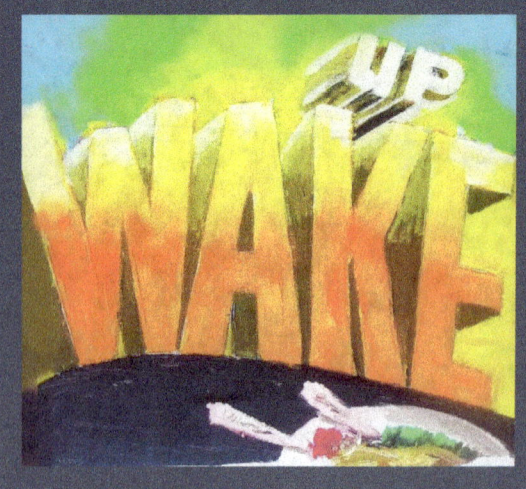

night of fun. "I want to go to Dreamland first," he said excitedly. Before he was able to go anywhere, he heard his sister Betty say, "Wake up sleepy head, dinner is ready." Samuel immediately thought about his night journey with his horse, and knew that was something he needed to do. "I need to go out to the barn first," Samuel, told her. He ran out to the barn to look for his trophies. He looked everywhere in the barn, and to his dismay, they were nowhere in sight. He went to Champion and asked, "Where did you hide the trophies?" All the horses just stared at him, shaking their heads. "He must have been dreaming," another horse said. Feeling sad, Samuel went back to the house to eat his dinner.

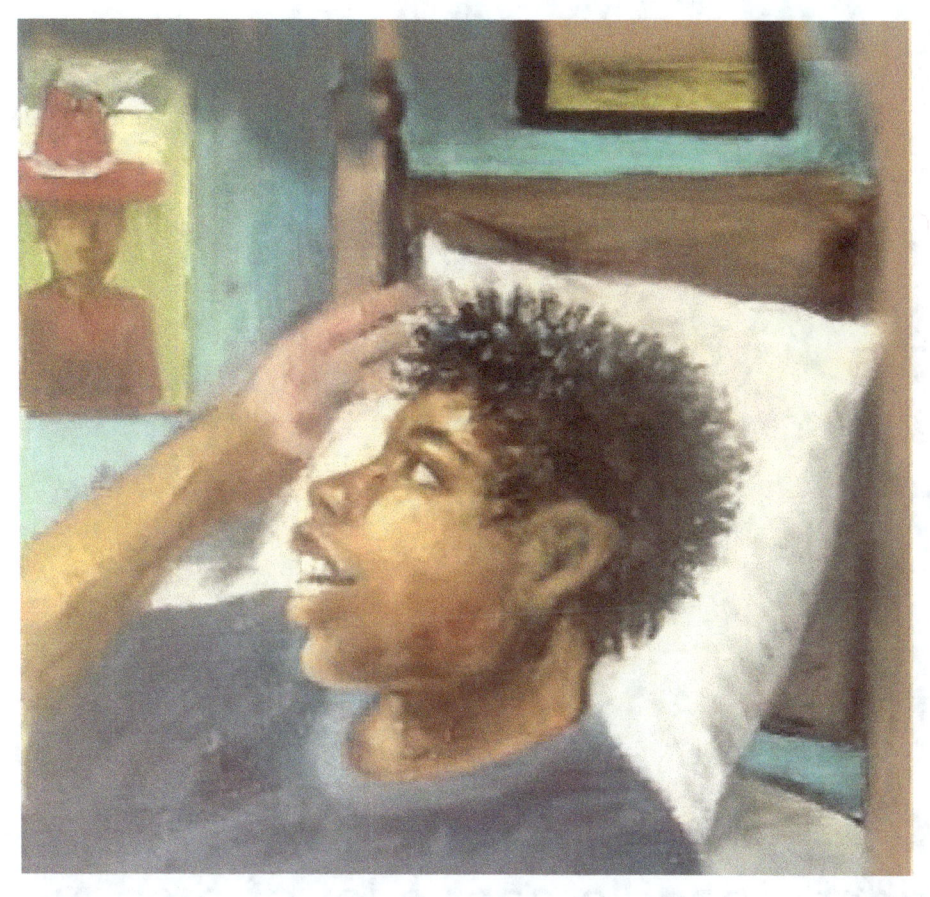

After eating, Bubble came into the room and jumped up on the top bunk bed, his favorite spot. While watching TV, Samuel told Bubble, "I would like to buy a bronc rider's saddle for Champion?" "Well, I read about the types of saddles that are good for horses when they compete in rodeos." "That would make you like a real cowboy." "Oh, yes, I definitely want to be like one and compete in rodeos with Champion."

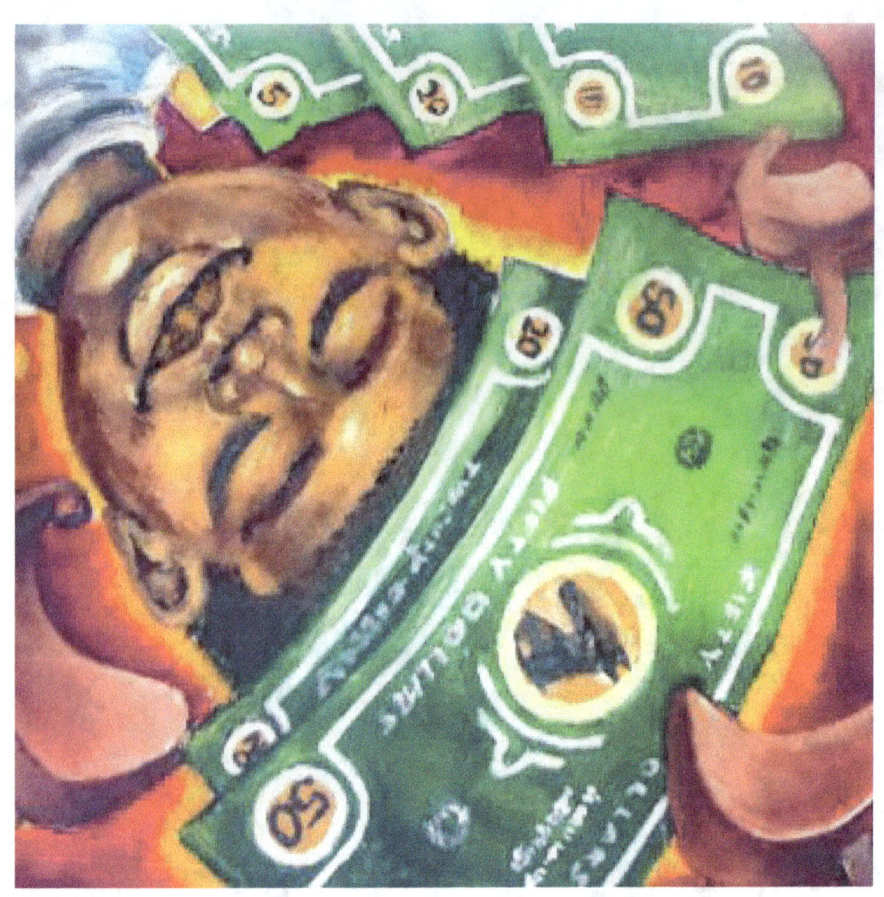

"You know that a bronc rider's saddle cost a lot of money. You do not even have a job, so you need to get one first," Bubble teased." "Okay, Bubble, I will ask dad for the money when he gets home from work tomorrow." "If you're brave enough, just go and ask him now, Bubble urged. Remembering when Champion told him to think positive, he hurried to ask his father's permission, and his father gladly said that he could get a part-time job.

Friday night,
Samuel told his
Parents about
Dreamland, and
about what Champion told him. If you go to
Dreamland, You must take your sisters and
brother, his father said. "Now do we believe
our son about Champion taking him to
Dreamland?" Bubble walked into the room, "I
believe he was just dreaming," he said. I do
too, Mary said. "Well," replied Carolyn, "I
believe him." Later, at midnight, they all got
up, dressed and ran out the house.

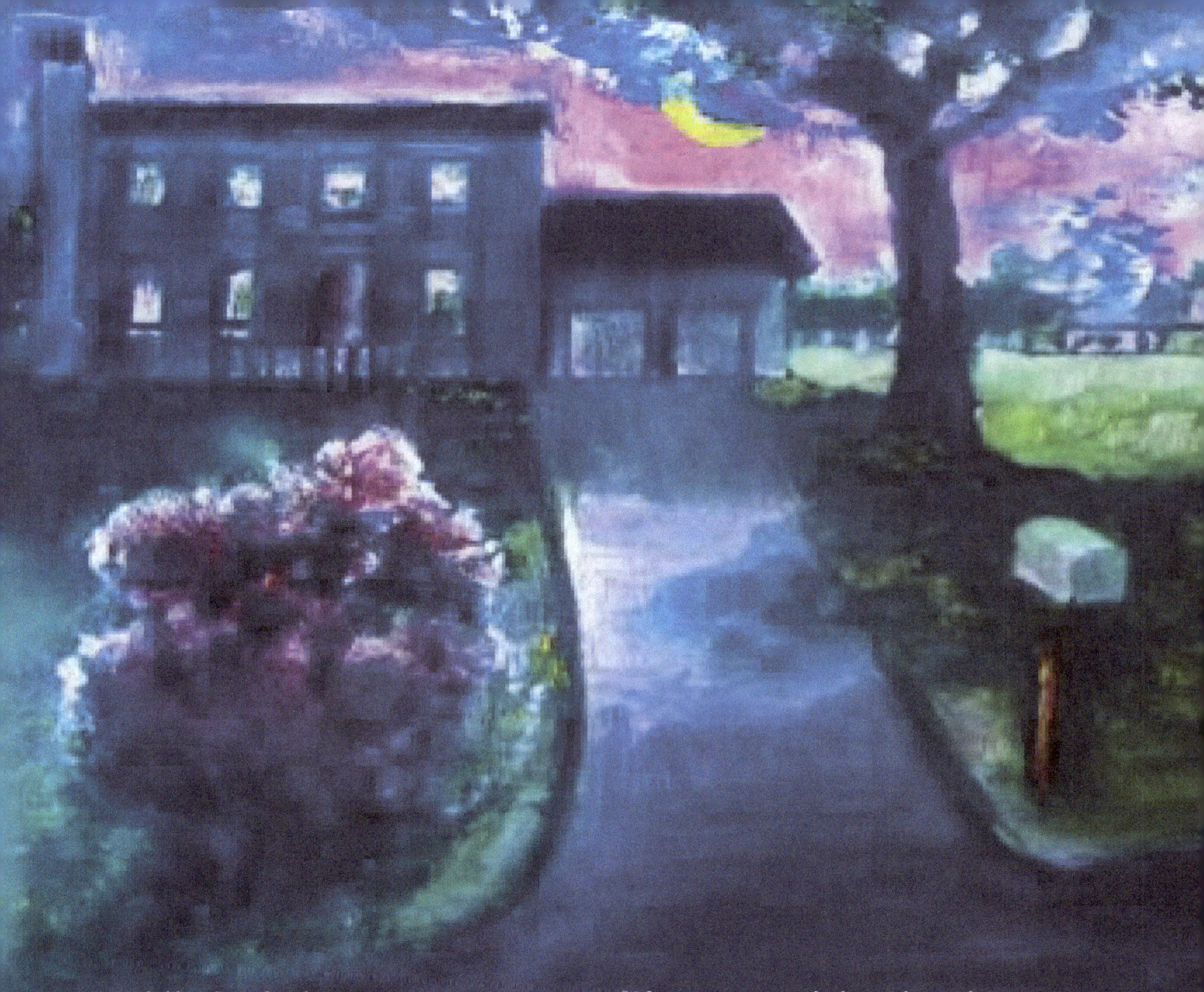

All their horses were waiting outside the barn with their wings spread out wide, ready to fly. "This is fantastic," Bubble, exclaimed, "our own airplanes ready to go." The girls stood and watched with excitement without saying a word. While mom and dad slept, they went out on the town that hot summer night.

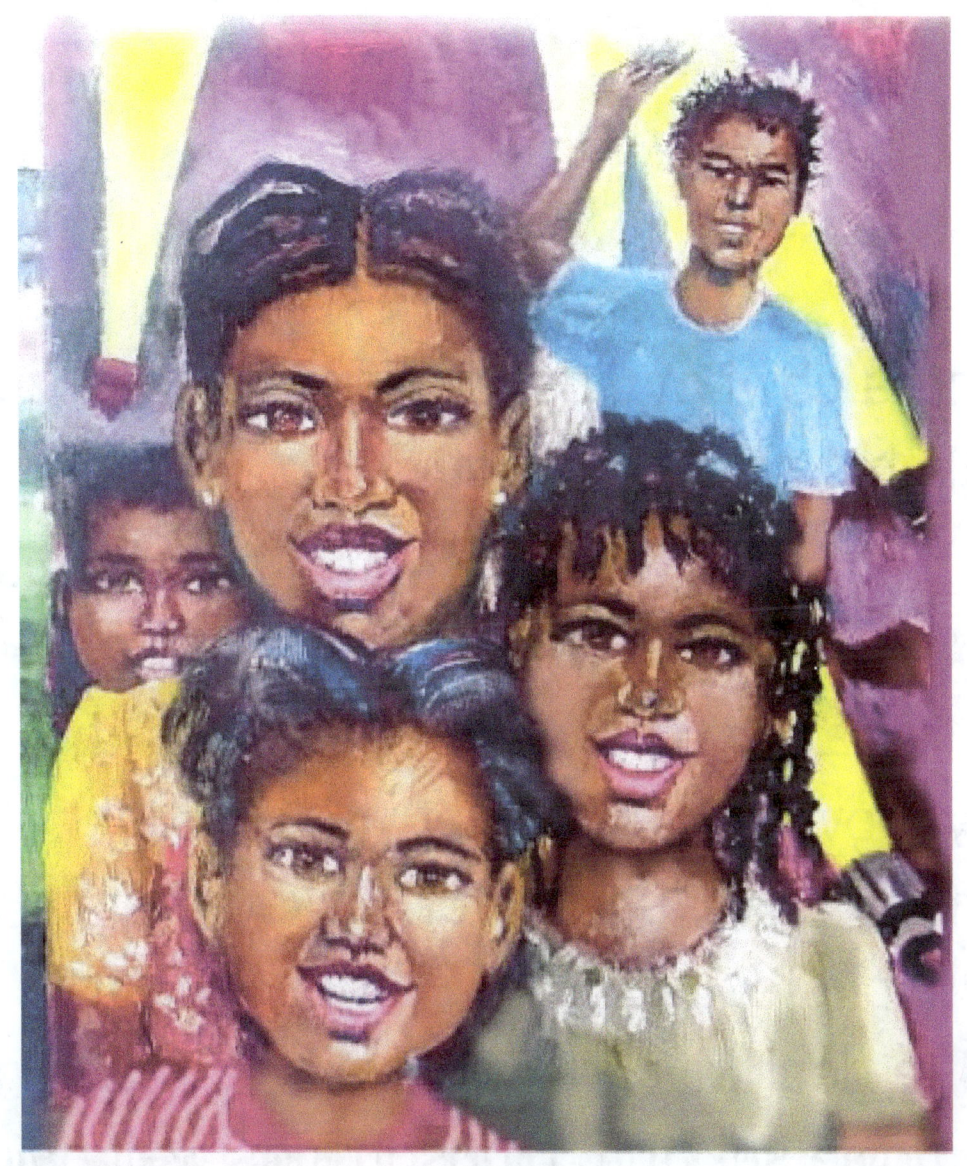

This where I was a few days ago, said Samuel. "Boy, no you were not, maybe in a dream," giggled Betty. "Let us go over there where they are shooting a movie," said Mary. "Well, maybe this might be our moment to make dad and mom proud," said Bubble. As they rode toward the movie set, there stood Tyler Perry.

Directing a cowboy scene. There were dozens of spotlights shining brightly.

 "Folks, look who we have here, the famous Johnson Family," said Mr. Perry." "How would you all like a part in the second half of this cowboy movie?" "Well what you all think," Carolyn the quiet, shy sister. Asked them. "Why not," Bubble replied. "Mr. Perry, you got yourself a deal with five superstars. That night on the movie set, the Johnson kids well paid after during a super job. Samuel knew he had more than enough money to buy as many saddles as he wanted.

Next, Samuel asked if anyone was ready to travel to Dreamland. They were all excited and ready to go to the place where horses came from, and dreams could come true with hard work and determination.

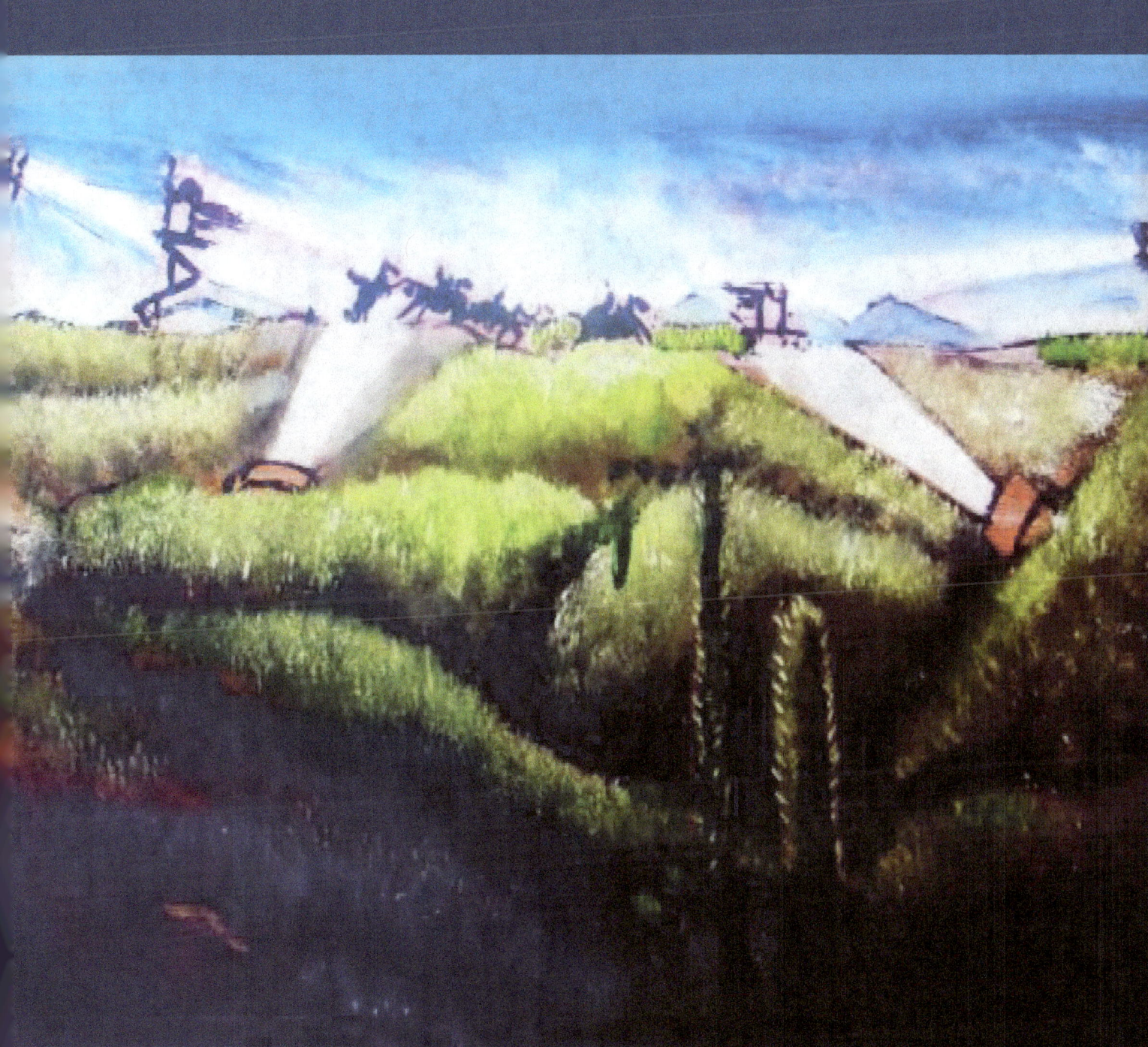

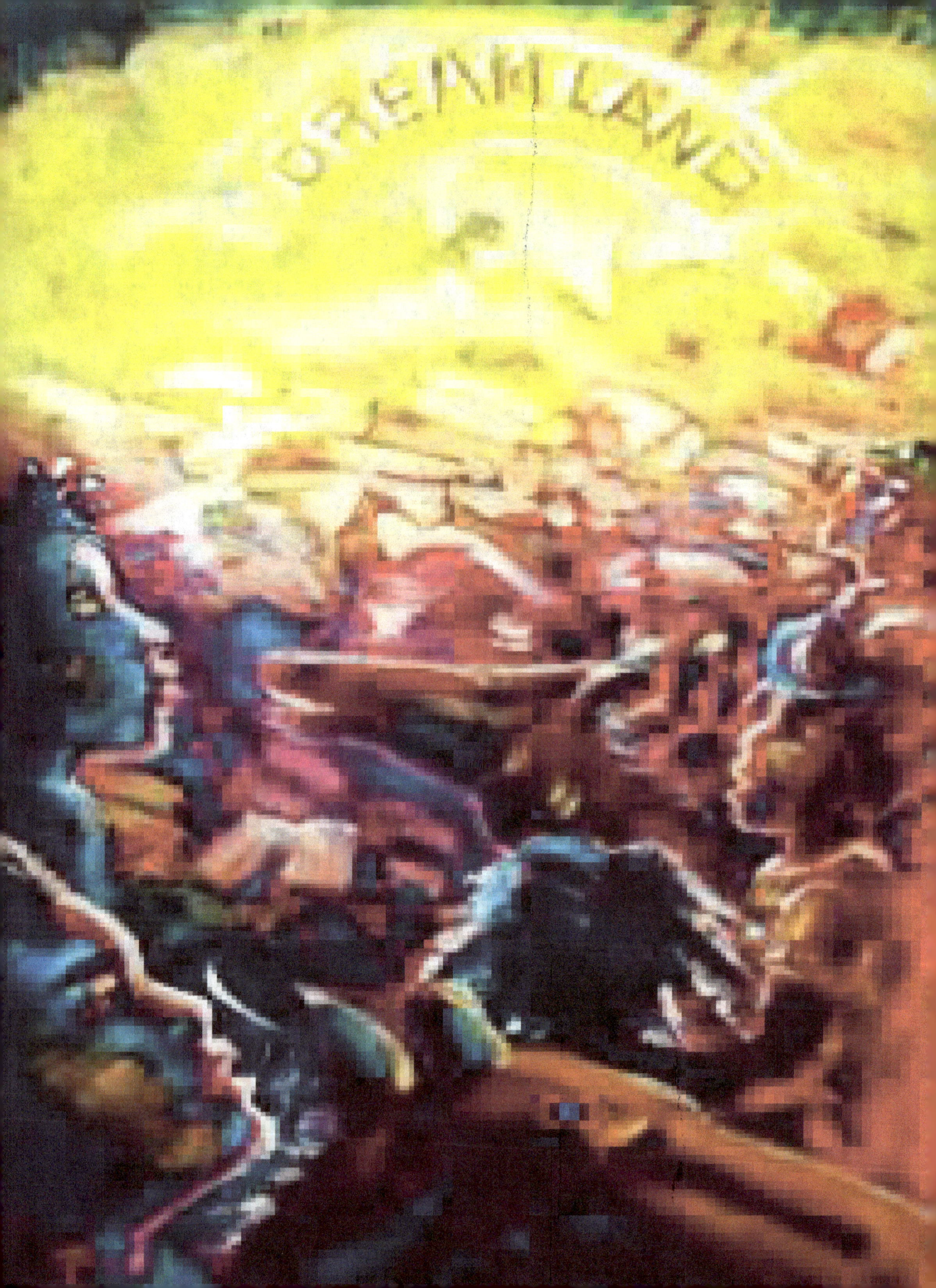

Off we went, riding our horses into dreamland World. We saw people asleep in their beds that night dreaming. Some dreams the people had were frightening, spooky, adventurous, and pleasant. Many were like us, rushing to get their dream before it disappeared when they awakened in the morning. A man came flying by us, hollering, "You have to find your dreams and hold onto them, do not let go." Soon a woman flew by, that is right, you can take it back and it is there when you wake up. Next, this kid flew by, "yes you can feel, touch, better your life and buy what you want. That night, we not only saw people chasing their dreams, but also animals, even cats, dogs, and yes horses, of course.

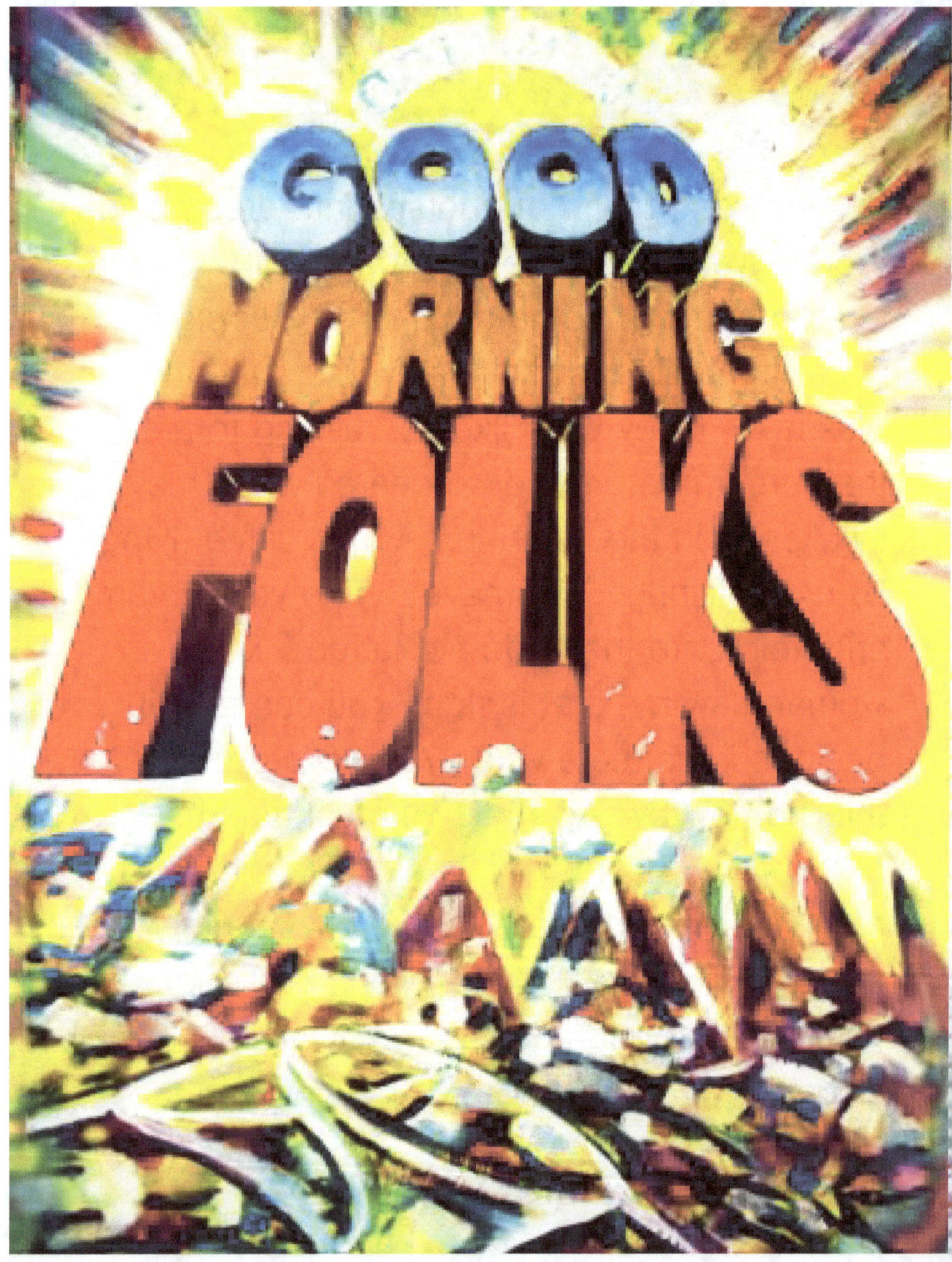

It has only been a few hours since they came to this wonderful place. Soon, they heard a very big booming voice speaking loudly. "Good morning folks, if you all want to keep and take your dreams home, you have to do three things. First, you must have a large goal, second, you have to be serious, and third, catch it with large nets, let no one stop you, and now go after your dreams."

They all flew in to catch their dreams with big wide fluffy nets. Samuel on Champion dashed like a bird, very high to catch his dream. Many folks stood on the sidelines cheering. They had no goals and did not want to go out to catch their dreams. Dogs and yes horses, of course, were sleeping as they flew in dreamland.

"Boy I'm tired and ready to go home," Samuel yelled, as he yawned. "Not so fast there little bro," said Bubble. "You got all you can carry, and I see one more I need to catch." "That is right," Betty yelled. And away they both went. Samuel sat by a large tree to rest, while Champion slept. Midnight was slowly coming and soon the sun would rise. "Let's go home now and get a few hours of sleep," yelled Bubble.

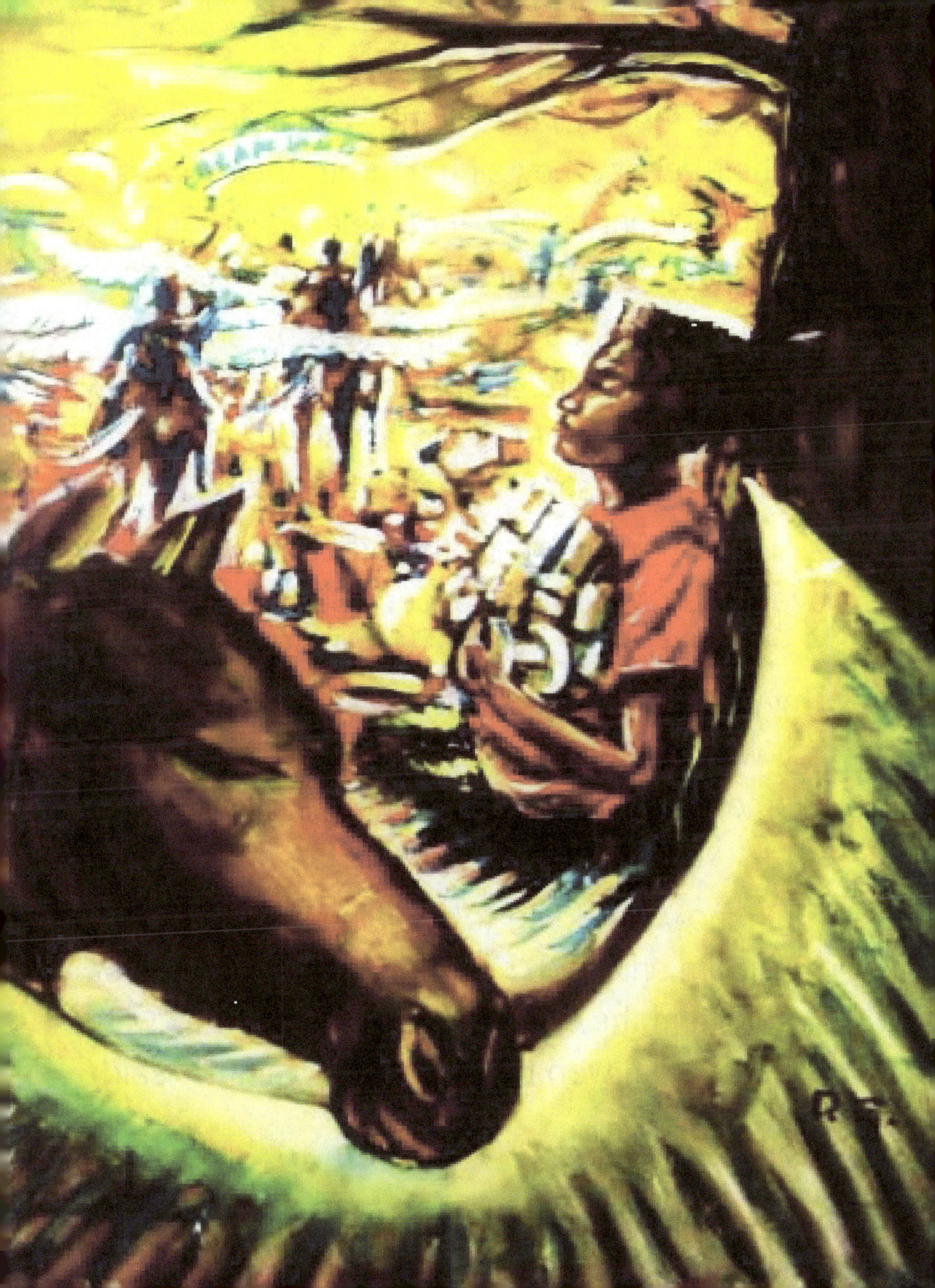

Back at the barn that night, with dream gifts in their hands, they all rushed to their rooms. Samuel went to bed with his arms around his dreams making sure they would not escape.

Bubble placed his game toys by an open window and fell asleep. Soon all of them flew out the window. However, his sisters held on to their games' toys in their room.

The next morning, the bright sun rose, everybody was happy except Bubble, his dream escaped. "Here big bro, I will share some of my dream toys, computers, and movie money with you," offered Carolyn. We all gave something to him, and a bright smile came on Bubble's face, now he is happy.

"Ok, how we going to explain what happened to mom and dad?" asked Mary. "We will just tell them the truth," said Samuel, "they will believe us, won't they?" "They might," said Betty.

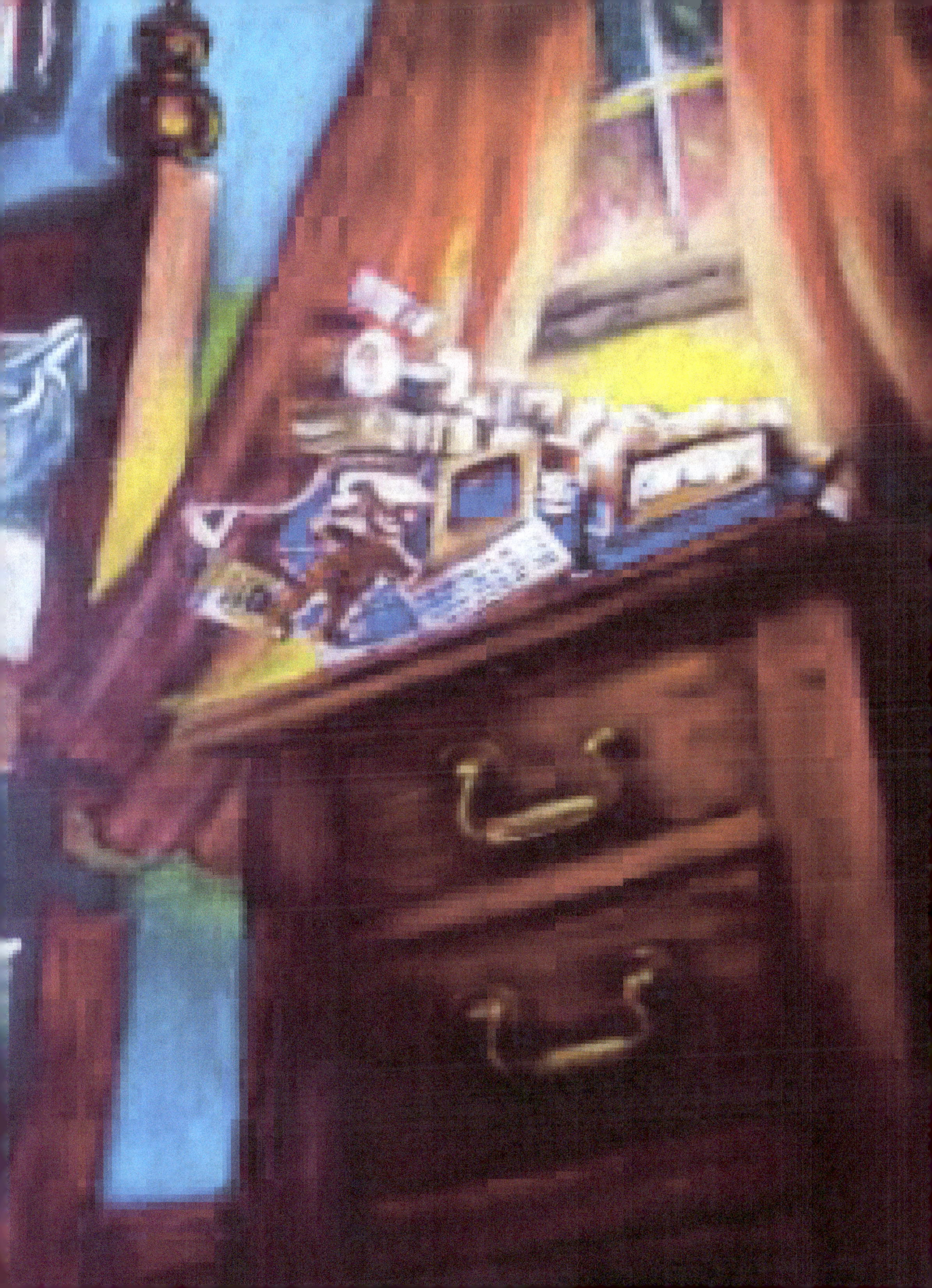

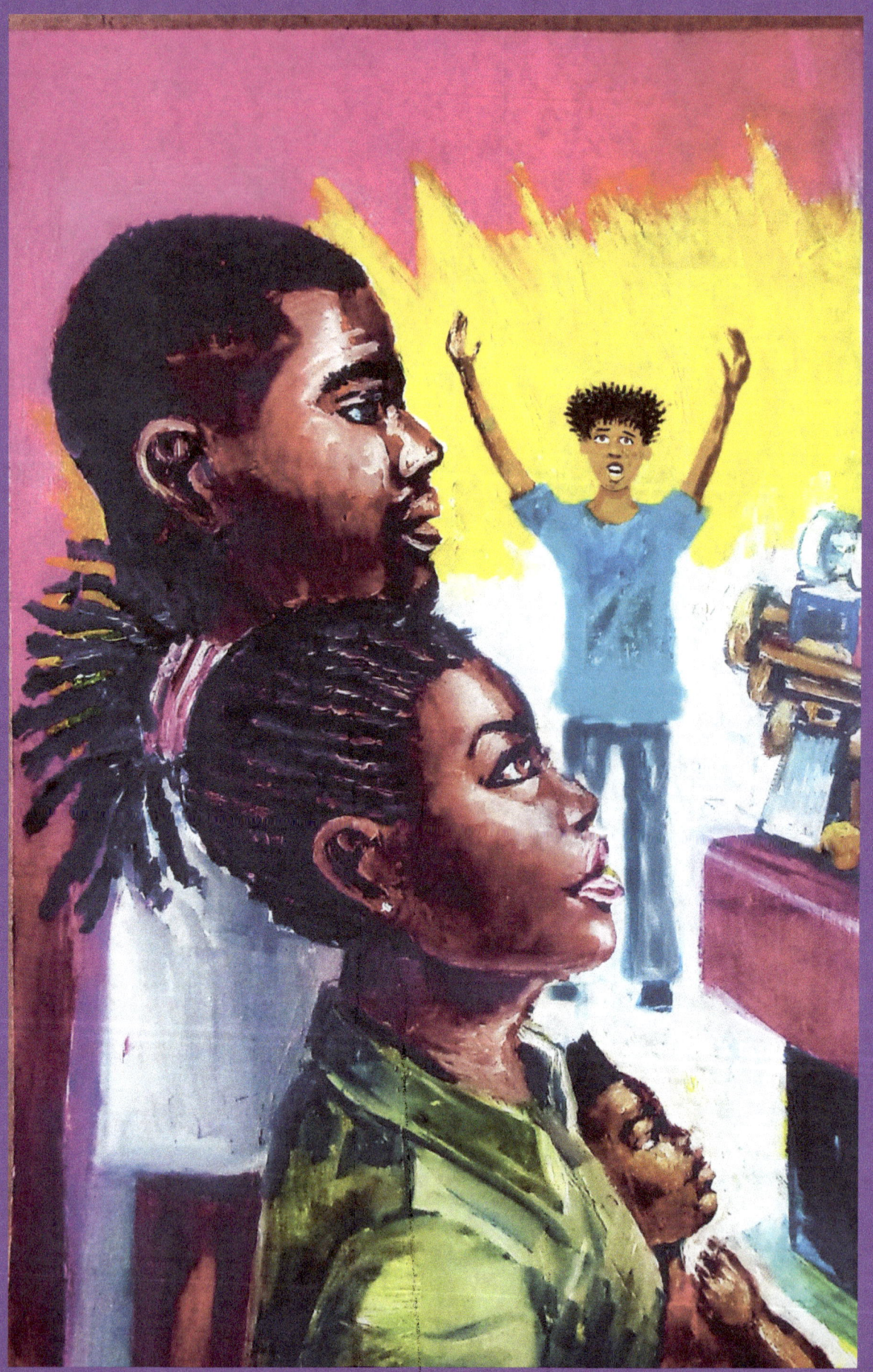

At breakfast, they told their parents about Dreamland. Mom laughed, "I heard about that place when I was a little girl but I have never been there." They all laughed, except dad, "look, I have never told your mother, but I have gone there." "How many times?" Samuel asked excitedly. "Maybe a dozen times," his father replied. Samuel was anxious to show his parents the dreams they had gotten and told them, "You will believe us when you see what we got in Dreamland, we will show you."

Upstairs, in the bedrooms, their parents could not believe their eyes. All the money, iPhones, toys, clothes, and computers surprised them. Bubble told them the whole story, when he finished talking they believe that it actually happened. My big brother just has a way with words, thought Mary, smiling.

"Maybe the old man that sold us those horses knew something," said father. Mother agreed,

"Yes honey, he wanted the kids to find out this secret themselves."

That weekend, they went to Green Stone Mall to shop, Samuel decided to wander around the Backyard Barn Store. Soon he saw large and small

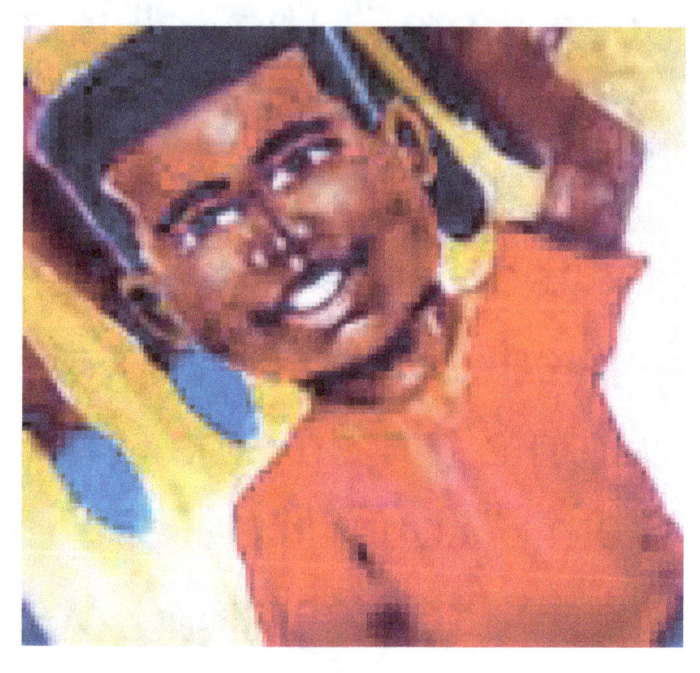

saddles displayed on a huge wall. A salesperson stated all the saddles were custom-made. Soon his parents walked in, "Which one do you want?" mom asked. "That tan bronc rider's saddle up at top," Samuel pointed out. "Well sir," that is what the young man wants," Dad said. Now dad was calling me a young man just like mom.

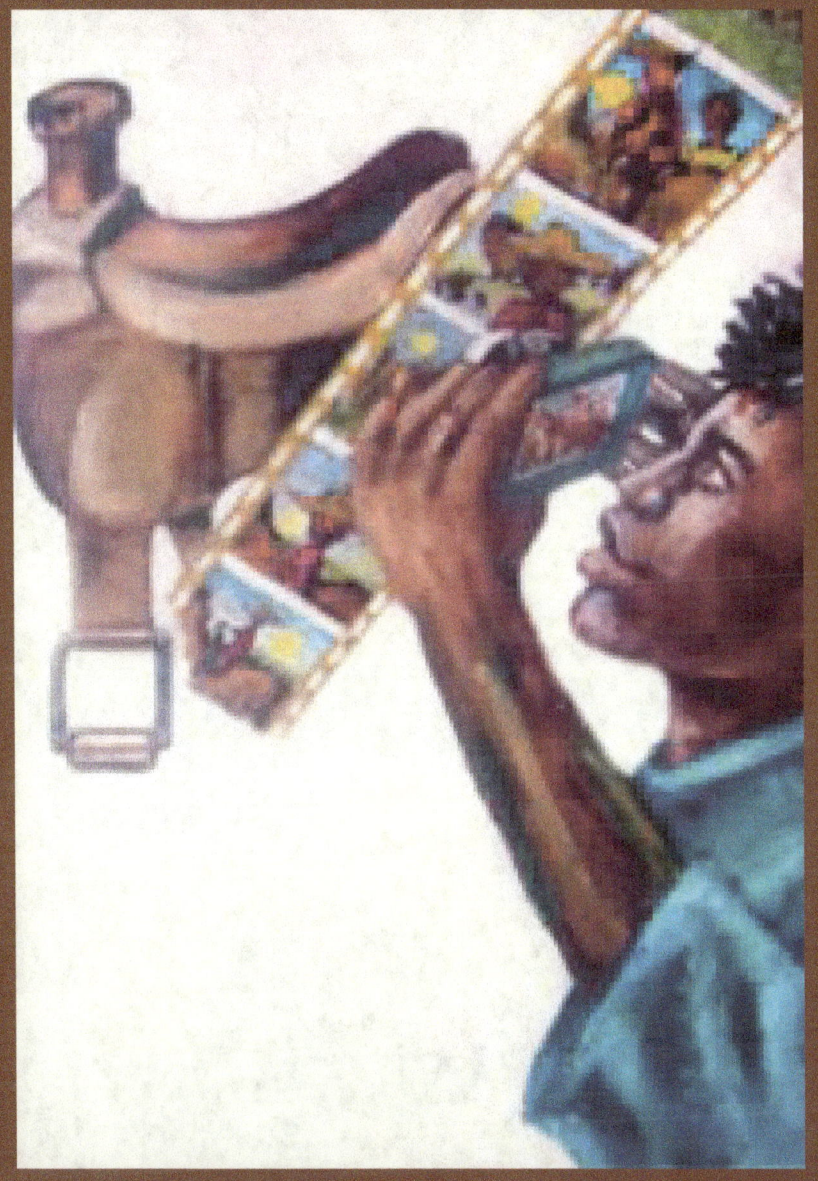

Samuel could not wait to get back home later that Saturday evening. He let dad put the saddle on Champion. Excited, he climbed up, and held onto the saddle, tightly. "Now you look like a super cool cowboy young man," dad said. Mom and the others came out to see him and Champion. Bubble filmed the festive occasion with his new camera.

Days later, Samuel rode with his brother and sisters on the back hills. "It seems we can only go to Dreamland at night," said Betty. "Yes," Mary said, but we should be able to go any time." As they were picking blackberries,

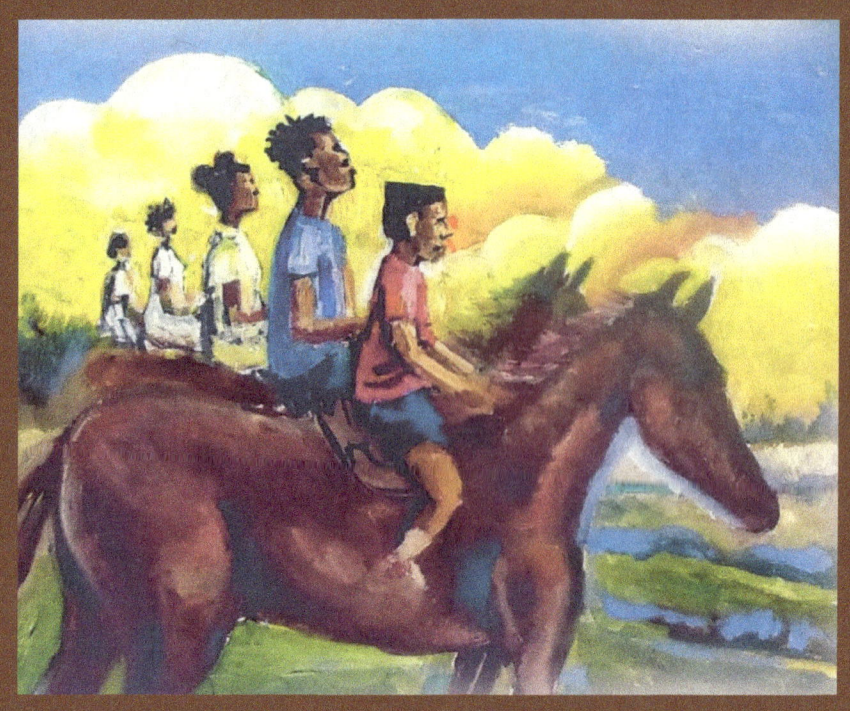

Carolyn had an idea, "Let's take mom and dad to Dreamland." "Well," said the horse, "you know it is only five of us horses, and seven of you." They went back home that

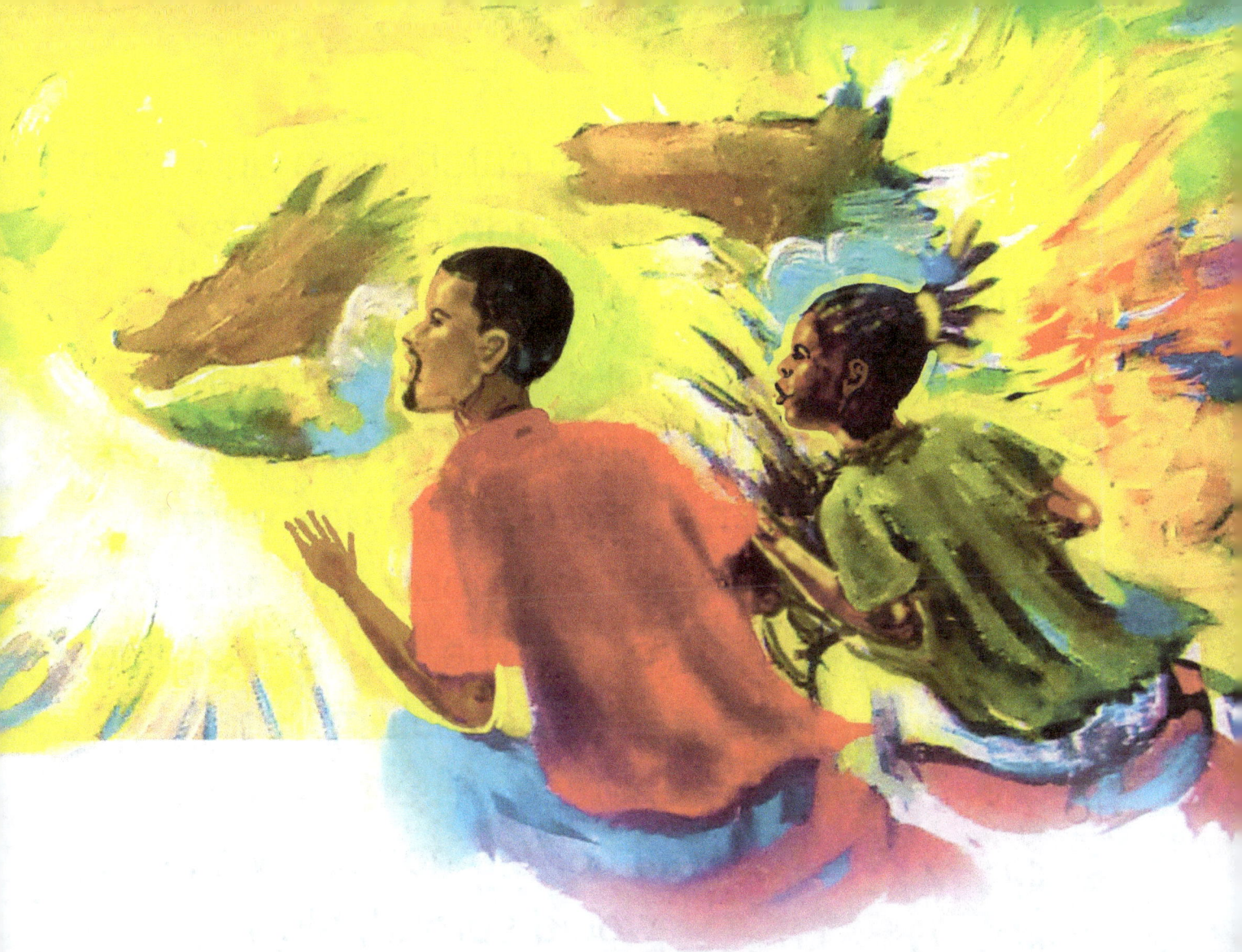

Evening, hoping their parent would go to Dreamland.

Fortunately, our parents were excited about going to our secret place, after they heard the horses talk. Bubble and Betty stayed behind that night while their parents went to Dreamland. They took the big wide fluffy nets and caught as many dreams as they could.

They joined in an effort to catch more and soon they were tired, and returned home before sunrise.

It was like a special holiday in our home the whole summer. Soon, from out of the dark green forest, our neighbors' kids rode up on their horses. Mom and Dad stood watching with 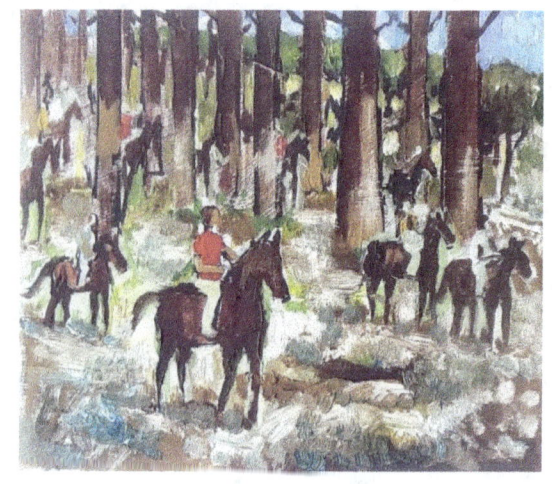 pride. The kids played and rode on their magical horses. All at the same time, the horses' wings would spread, slowly lifting them up toward the bright sky. Now, the kids really enjoy traveling and learning a lot about other places. Samuel and Champion have competed in many rodeos and have successfully won many more trophies; they are certainly seeing their dreams come true. As Tyler Perry says, "Anything you want is possible."

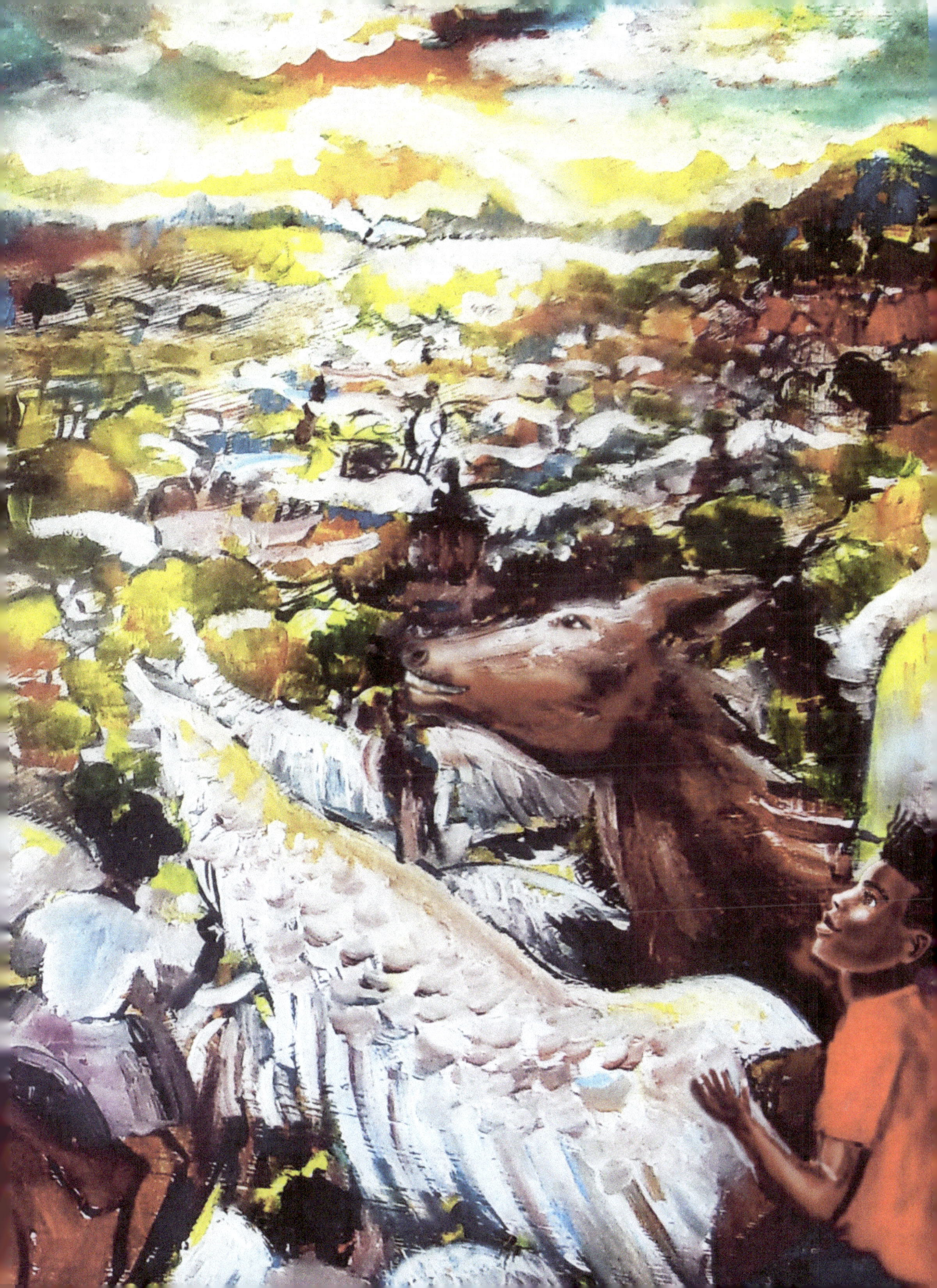